INTRODUCTION

Welcome back to FastTrack™!

Hope you enjoyed Drums 2 and are ready to play some hits. Have you and your friends formed a band? Or do you feel like jamming with the CD? Either way, make sure you're relaxed and comfortable…it's time to play!

As always, don't try to bite off more than you can chew. If your arms are tired, take some time off. If you get frustrated, put down your sticks, sit back and just listen to the CD. If you forget a technique or rhythm, go back and learn it. If you're doing fine, think about finding an agent.

CONTENTS

ABOUT THE CD

Again, you get a CD with the book! Each song in the book is included on the CD, so you can hear how it sounds and play along when you're ready.

Each example on the CD is preceded by one measure of "clicks" to indicate the tempo and meter. Pan right to hear the drum part emphasized. Pan left to hear the accompaniment emphasized.

7777 W. BLUEMOUND RD. P.O. BOX 13819 MILWAUKEE, WI 53213

Visit Hal Leonard online at
www.halleonard.com

LEARN SOMETHING NEW EACH DAY

We know you're eager to play, but first we need to explain a few new things. We'll make it brief—only one page...

Melody and Lyrics

There's that extra musical staff again! Remember, this additional staff (on top) shows you the song's melody and lyrics. This way, you can follow along more easily as you play your accompaniment part, whether you're playing, resting or showing off with a solo . . . well, sometimes drummers do get a solo.

And if you happen to be playing with a singer, this new staff is their part.

Endings

In case you've forgotten some of the **ending symbols** from Songbook 1, here's a reminder:

1st and 2nd Endings

These are indicated by brackets and numbers:

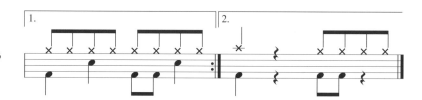

Simply play the song through to the first ending, then repeat back to the first repeat sign, or beginning of the song (whichever is the case). Play through the song again, but skip the first ending and play the second ending.

D.S. al Coda

When you see these words, go back and repeat from this symbol: 𝄋

Play until you see the words "To Coda" then skip to the Coda, indicated by this symbol: ⊕

Now just finish the song.

That's about it! Enjoy the music...

All Day and All of the Night

Words and Music by Ray Davies

be with you all of the ___ time. All day   and all of the night. _   All day   and

all of the night. _   All day   and all of the night. _

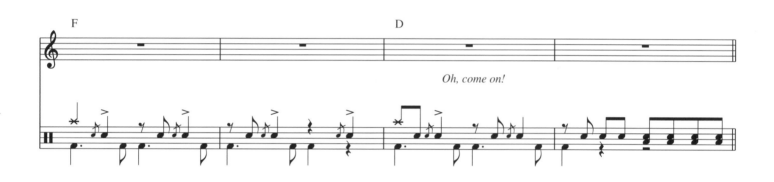

Oh, come on!

Guitar Solo

D.S. al Coda

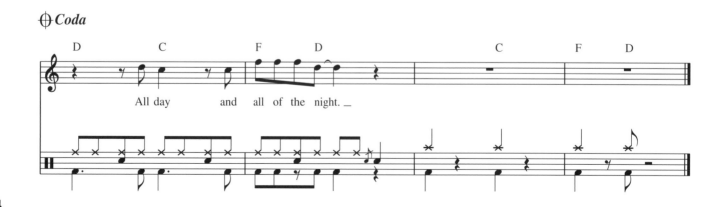

Coda

All day   and all of the night. _

② Best of My Love

Words and Music by John David Souther, Don Henley and Glenn Frey

Verse

6

cold dark cloud ___ that we could nev-er rise a-bove. ___ But

here in my heart ___ I give you the best ___ of my ___ love. Oh, _____

Chorus

___ sweet dar - lin, you get the best of my
(You get the best of my ___ love.)

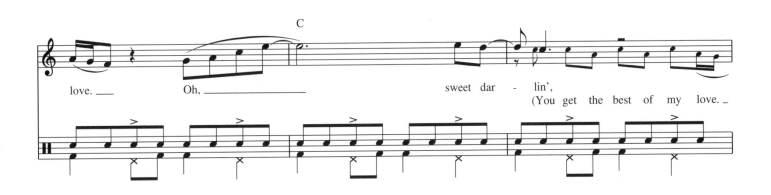

love. ___ Oh, _____ sweet dar - lin', you get the best of my love. __
(You get the best of my love. _

Bridge

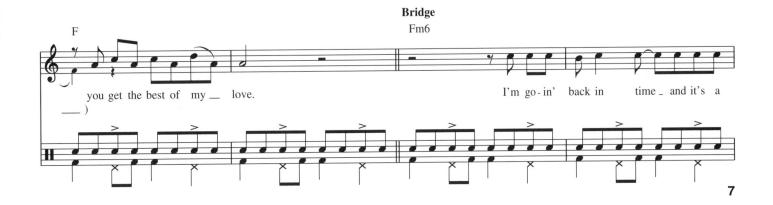

you get the best of my ___ love. I'm go-in' back in time ___ and it's a
___)

7

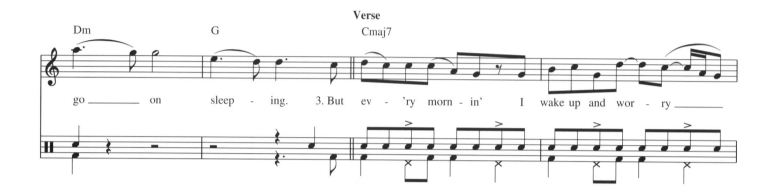

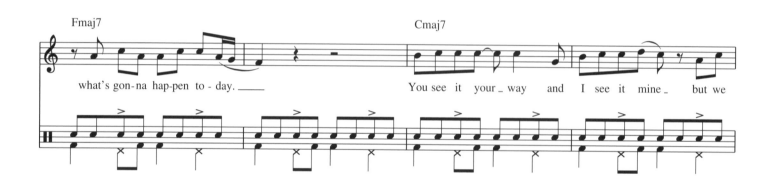

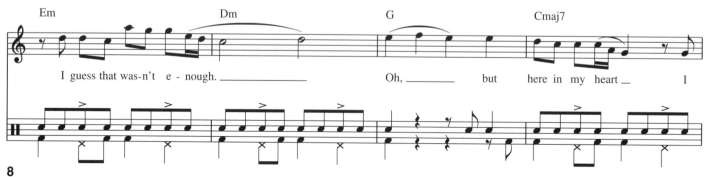

Day Tripper

Words and Music by John Lennon and Paul McCartney

Interlude

Day trip-per.

Day trip-per, yeah. ——

Day trip-per.

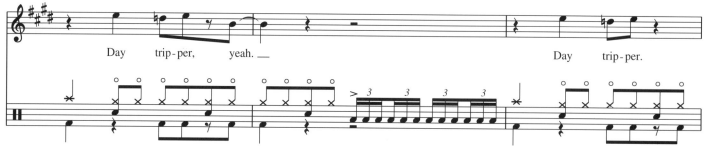

Day trip-per, yeah. ——

4 Hey Joe

Words and Music by Billy Roberts

Alright! Shoot one more time again, will ya?

Interlude

D.S. al Coda

Alright!

⊕ *Coda*

I'm go-in' way down south, ___ way down ___ where I ___ ___ can be free. Ain't but one ___ lit-tle fight.

⑤ I Shot the Sheriff

Words and Music by Bob Marley

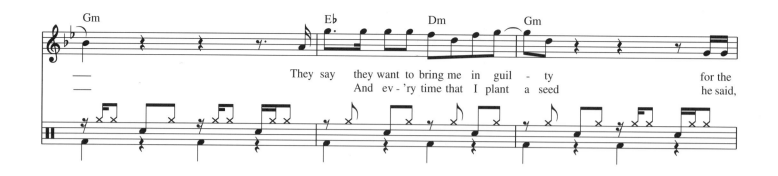

They say they want to bring me in guil-ty for the
And ev-'ry time that I plant a seed he said,

kill-ing of a dep — u — ty. ___ For the life ___ of a dep — u — ty. ___
"Kill it be-fore it grows."___ He said, "Kill ___ it be-fore it grows."

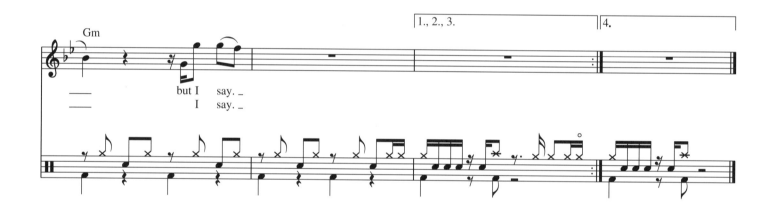

but I say. _
I say. _

| 1., 2., 3. | 4. |

Additional Lyrics

3. I shot the sheriff
   But I swear it was in self-defense.
   I shot the sheriff
   But I swear it was in self-defense.
   Freedom came my way one day
   And I started out down there.
   All of a sudden I see sheriff John Brown.
   Aiming to shoot me down.
   So I shot, I shot him down.
   And I say...

4. I shot the sheriff
   But I did not shoot the deputy.
   I shot the sheriff
   But I didn't shoot the deputy.
   Reflexes got the better of me.
   And what is to be must be.
   Every day the bucket goes to the well,
   But one day the bottom will drop out.
   Yes, one day the bottom will drop out.
   And I say...

Miss You

Words and Music by Mick Jagger and Keith Richards

Won't you come home? Come home!

Ah.

Ti - ki - ti ti - ki - ti ti - ki - ti ti - ki.

I've been walk-ing Cen - tral Park,

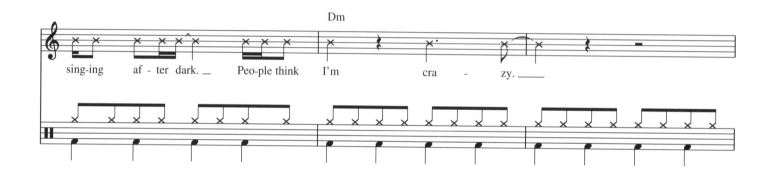

sing-ing af - ter dark. _ Peo-ple think I'm cra - zy. ____

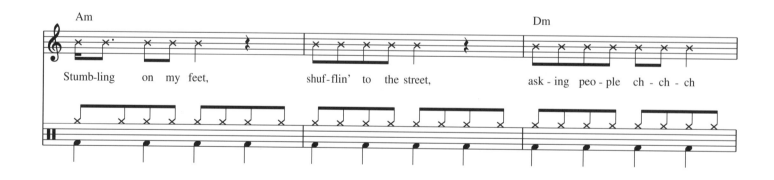

Stumb-ling on my feet, shuf-flin' to the street, ask - ing peo - ple ch - ch - ch

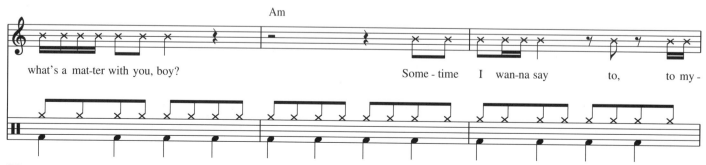

what's a mat-ter with you, boy? Some - time I wan-na say to, to my-

22

Outro-Chorus

7 Smoke on the Water

Words and Music by Ritchie Blackmore, Ian Gillan, Roger Glover, Jon Lord and Ian Paice

Verse

Gm

1. We all came out to Mon - treaux on the
2. They burned down the gam - bling house. It
3. We ended up at the Grand Hotel.

F   Gm

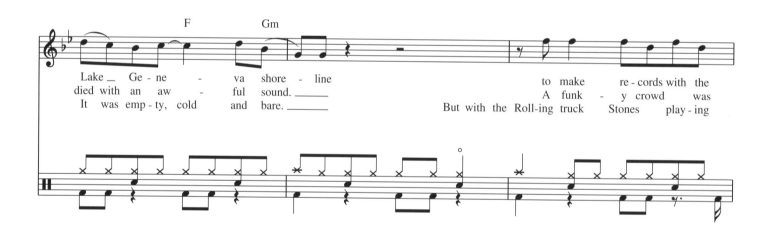

Lake __ Ge - ne - va shore - line to make re - cords with the
died with an aw - ful sound. _____ A funk - y crowd was
It was emp - ty, cold and bare. _____ But with the Roll - ing truck Stones play - ing

F   Gm

mo - bile. We did - n't have much time. _
run - ning in and out, pull - ing kids off the ground.
just out - side mak - ing our mu - sic there. With a

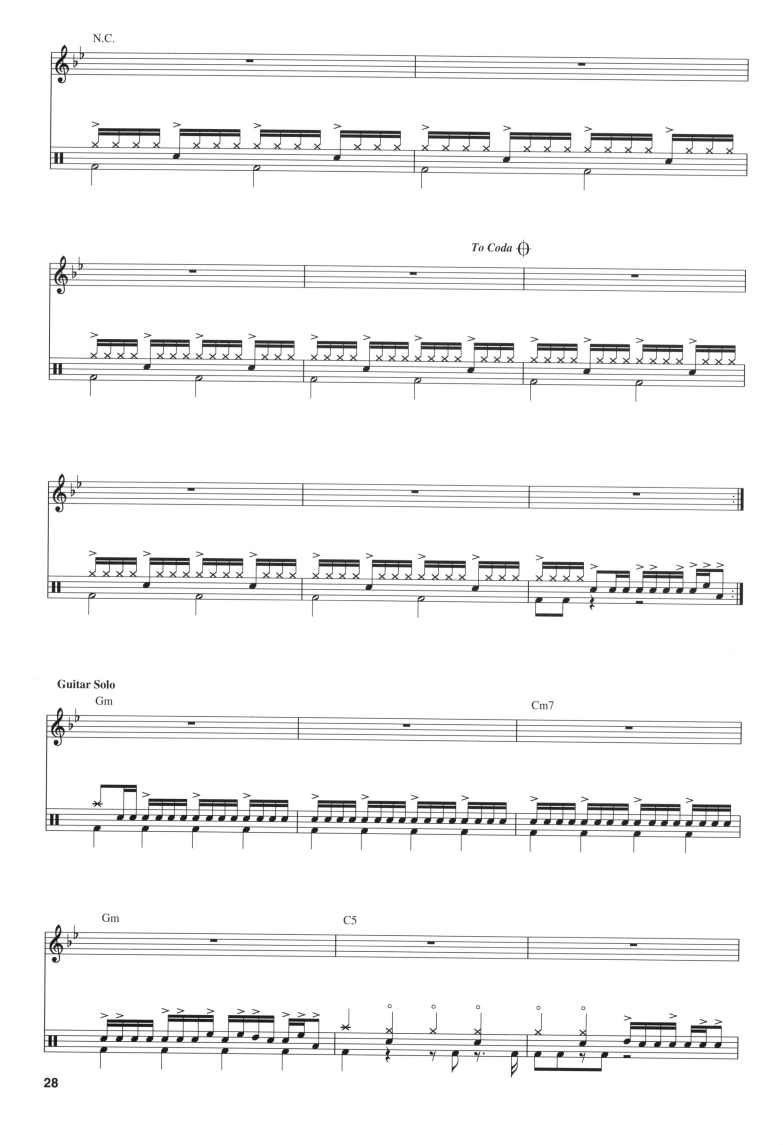

N.C.

To Coda ⊕

Guitar Solo

Gm   Cm7

Gm   C5

Surfin' U.S.A.

Written by Chuck Berry and Brian Wilson

Ven-tu-ra Coun-ty Line, __ San-ta Cruz __ and Tress - els, __
Pa-ci-fic Pal-i - sades, __ San O-no-fre and Sun - set, __

Aus-tra-lia's Nar-a - bine. __ All o - ver Man-hat - tan __
Re-don-do Beach L. A. __ All o - ver La Jol - la __

and down Do-he-ny way. __ } Ev-'ry-bod-y's gone surf - in', __
at Wal-a-me-a Bay. __ }

Keyboard Solo

(1st time only)

surf-in' U. S. A. __ 2. We'll all be plan-ning out a